ALL-NIGHT LINGO TANGO

PITT POETRY SERIES

Ed Ochester, Editor

ALL-NIGHT
LINGO TANGO

Barbara Hamby

UNIVERSITY OF PITTSBURGH PRESS

Published by the University of Pittsburgh Press, Pittsburgh, Pa., 15260

Manufactured in the United States of America

Printed on acid-free paper

10 9 8 7 6 5 4 3 2 1

ISBN 13: 978-0-8229-6017-1

ISBN 10: 0-8229-6017-6

for Phyllis Moore—
quick step artist
extraordinaire
in the
lingo tango,
with love

Contents

I

Ode to Anglo Saxon, Film Noir, and the Hundred Thousand Anxieties that Plague Me like Demons in a Medieval Christian Allegory, *3*

Who Do Mambo, *5*

Working at Pam-Pam's, *7*

Ode on Laundry, Lester Young, and Your Last Letter, *9*

9 Sonnets from the Psalms, *11*

A Birdman to You, Baby, *16*

Ode to Airheads, Hairdos, Trains to and from Paris, *18*

Mambo Cadillac, *20*

O'ahu Mambo, *22*

II

LINGO SONNETS

Aloha, Dad, Au Revoir, Goodbye, *27*

Betty Boop's Bebop, *28*

Caliban Passes His Driving Test on the Ninth Try, *29*

Desdemona Resuscitated by Sir John Falstaff, EMT, *30*

Elizabeth Cady Stanton Writes the Dictionary, *31*

Friday Slams Crusoe, *32*

Ganymede's Dream of Rosalind, *33*

Hope Revived: The Road to Baghdad, *34*

I Find an Entrance to Hell, *35*

Jane Austen Rewrites *Hamlet* with Interruptions by Russian Poets, *36*

Karen, David, and I Stop across the Street from the Pitti Palace, *37*

Lysistrata Lectures the Gods, *38*

Mr. Nollie Hinton Talks to Me while I Test-Drive His 1955 Studebaker, 39

Nietzsche Explains the Übermensch to Lois Lane, 40

Olive Oyl Thinks about Quantum Theory, 41

Punk Puck or Robin Goodfellow with Fender Stratocaster, 42

Queen Mab Blues or Quick, Run for Cover, She's Reading Horace Again, 43

Raskolnikov Rates the Plays, 44

So Says Cleopatra, Reincarnated as a Hippie Chick, circa 1967, 45

Titus Woos Titania, 46

Ulysses Talks with Freud about the Underworld, 47

Venus and Dogsbody, a Match Made in New Jersey, 48

Whatever or *As You Like It*, Part Two, 49

Xerox My Heart, Three-Headed Dog, 50

Yorick's Soliloquy, 51

Zeus, It's Your Leda, Sweetie Pie, 52

III

All-Night Lingo Tango, 55

Ode on Dictionaries, 57

Ode to Odor, Ardor, and the Queen's Chickabobboo, 59

Ode to Diagramming Sentences in Eighth-Grade English Class
with Moonlight, Drugs, and Stars, 61

Ode on My 45s, Insomnia, and My Poststructuralist Superego, 63

Ode to Fear, 65

Ode on Cake, Catcalls, Eggs with a Minor Scary Reference
to the End of the World, 67

Ode to Little Boys, 69

Ode to White Peaches, Pennies, Planets, and Bijou, the Dog, 72

Ode on the Letter *M*, 74

Notes, 77

Acknowledgments, 79

Lord,

    I give thanks to You for all of this babble of life, in which
I am drowning since the beginning of time without hope of rescue

    a bean counter focused on an endless search for nothing.

           "Breviary,"
           Zbigniew Herbert

Ode to Anglo Saxon, Film Noir, and the Hundred Thousand Anxieties that Plague Me like Demons in a Medieval Christian Allegory

Yo, Viking dudes, who knew your big dog cock-of-the-walk
    raping and pillaging would put us all here, right smack
dab in the middle of a decade filled with the stink
    of war? Yes, sir, boys and girls, we're eating an old sock
sandwich, but we're speaking English, kind of a weird fluke
    (a piece of luck, not the parasite), because the kick-
ass Angles were illiterate hicks while the sublime Greeks
    had been writing poetry for a thousand years, heck,
history and philosophy, too, though they did shellac
    the Trojans and a lot of other guys as well, stuck
them with their Bronze Age swords, testosterone run amok,
    or so I'm thinking here from my present perch—a swank
appartement à Paris, swilling champagne, clothes black,
    as if my past were *un chef d'oeuvre* by Jan van Eyck,
the soundtrack written by Johann Sebastian Bach
    or his son, rather than the Three Stooges-Lawrence Welk
debacle that really occurred. My mind's a train wreck
    of two lingoes, twenty-six letters, and thousands of quick
images from movies, French—yes, but mostly *aw-shucks-
    ma'am* Hollywood Westerns or *policiers* in stark
black and white, and I'm the twist, tomato, skirt, the weak
    sister who rats out her grifter boyfriend, palms a deck
of Luckies she puffs while scheming with the private dick
    to pocket twenty large, or I'm the classy dame, sick
of her stinking rich life and her Ralph Bellamy schmuck

of a boyfriend. That's when Bogart's three-pack-a-day croak
(dialogue by Raymond Chandler) sounds like music,
    maybe John Coltrane, and you're up the five-and-dime creek,
ma chère, because love can turn you into a mark, punk,
    jingle-brained two-bit patsy who'd take a fast sawbuck
for snitching out her squeeze to the cops. Or you're the crack
    whore with an MBA standing on the corner in chic
Versace rags, falling for the DA till the Czech
    drug lord plugs him. So who are you? Not the hippie chick
of your early twenties or the Sears and Roebuck
    Christian judge your mother became, though Satan still stalks
you on a regular basis. Is that guy a slick
    operator or what with his Brylcreemed hair and pock-
marked face? There's still smallpox in Hell, so you push him back
    whenever you can, grow orchids and for dinner cook
risotto alla Milanese, because *knick, knack*
    paddy whack, you're counting on something, not luck or rock
and roll, though you've been there—at the HIC with Mick
    Jagger prancing around like a hopped-up jumping jack
on speed. No, *ma petite* Marcella Proust, this is the joke:
    when your mother prays for you, your stuttering heart ticks
a little more like a Swiss-made watch, and when you speak,
    does French come out? Nah, it's the echo of those shock-jock
Vikings, hacking their way across Europe, red-haired, drunk
    on blood and blondes, and though your husband looks like the Duke
of Cambridge, that's not what you love so much, ya dumb cluck,
    but his Henry James-Groucho Marx-Cajun shtick. Knock,
knock. Who's there? It's Moe, Larry, and Curly, nyuk nyuk nyuk.

Who Do Mambo

A sports writer complained to Joe Louis about another boxer who didn't like to take punches to the body. Louis replied, "Who do?"

Mon Dieu, said the Hindoo, *I don't want to stop drinking.* Who do?
　　But sometimes you have to put down your glass so you
can pick it up for another round. At the University Ladies' Tea
　　with the pill-popping dean's wife and Marxist shrews,
you don't want to talk to them or anyone else. Who do?
　　But like Audrey Hepburn in *My Fair Lady* you say
How do you do, call on Andrew Marvell and George Herbert
　　to rescue you, but you draw the short straw,
and there's Julie Andrews in *The Sound of Music* with her igloo
　　smile and Christmas sweater. You are the Sioux
in this cavalry charge, and you need some firewater pronto,
　　gin and lighter fluid or a gun, but that's so American,
and who would you shoot but yourself, so you try to spin some voodoo
　　around this vampire soirée. Where are the chicken bones
and bat fangs when you need them, Miss Nancy Drew?
　　Face facts, you don't have a clue. Let me preview
my upcoming bout of spinal meningitis for you,
　　or shall I invoke Bob Dylan, mathematician and Hebrew
troubadour, for I am tangled up in glue or something like it, goo
　　or ooze. If I were a cow, I'd be bigger than I am, say moo
and pray to Shiva, but as it is, I am a fourth-rate kangaroo
　　praying for rescue in a bottle, my mind a zoo,
a giraffe popping out my left ear, a zebra out my right. Whew,
　　that hurt, but so much does these days. *Much Ado*
About Nothing, that's my play, Beatrice and crew. Let's review.

Everything I adore is either forbidden to me or taboo,
which is pretty much the same thing. O Alice, I grew
    an inch with that one, or was it my nose? Hey, Pinocchio, you
want me to chop you for firewood? Who do? Wait, I have a few
    things to say about hue. I'm orange but, *carissimo*, you
are as blue as you were the day Picasso, or was it Braque, drew
    you in Montmartre in the Bateau Lavoir, and now that my shoe
is wedged in my mouth again and my underpants askew,
    I'll take this opportunity to bid you an affectionate adieu.
Parting is such sweet sorrow that I would pitch some woo
    with you till next Wednesday; O Shiva, the queue
to your divine brain is teeming with supplicants, so in lieu
    of the old one-two, I'll sign off. Something nasty just blew
in from Kazakhstan, and my electric bill's twenty years overdue.
    Mirror, mirror on the wall—Oh, God, not you.

Working at Pam-Pam's

Ava, darling, skin white as mayonnaise, eyes of cat-scratch topaz,
    zirconia smile, making *Mogambo* with Gable in Africa,
Bwana Clark, to you, baby, Grace Kelly tumbling the substitute daddy,
    you rolling in Swamp Sinatra. What did you see in him—dumb
crooner from Hoboken, a shrimp, and you in a gal's biggest fix,
    x- and y-chromosomes splitting in your deepest beauty, that toxic
ditch of burping and feeding on the horizon. You think you know
    what the years ahead hold—you left with the baby, Sinatra a cad.
Enemies or lovers—who's to say? Does anyone really change? Henry V,
    Vlad the Impaler, Saint Teresa of Avila—some do, but some
feel sucking the blood from a maiden's neck is all they can manage. You
    understood how beauty could take you only so far. Of course, if
God were in his heaven, we all might be film goddesses rather than fat
    timecard-punching factory workers with lacquered beehives, sewing
halter tops for girls whose primary job will always be painting their nails.
    Such a world begs you to believe in the Hindu idea of *maya,* which
is to say everything is illusion, kind of like the movies or theater or
    remember the time you found your boyfriend with your best friend? I
jump at the idea of *maya,* because though I try to be good, right on cue
    quick as a bunny, the devil pulls me into his Buick, and the DJ
keeps playing "Who Do You Love?" Ava, you started out as a bit player: carhop,
    pretty hatcheck girl, ringsider, and then your gorgeous face was stuck
like candy on magazines and marquees from Sacramento to Buffalo,
    Orlando to Natchez. When you lay dying in London, did you feel
more alive than ever or was it like the story of Vishnu and the holy man
    Narada, who asks the god for the secret of *maya?* Vishnu says to him,
"Narada, dive into that lake," which he does and emerges a princess, slim,

married to a powerful king. Her life is golden. She has many children,
owns palaces, her children have children, but her father and husband quarrel,

   lash out at each other until all her family lie dead on the battlefield. No
person has known such grief. Her dear ones lie on the funeral pyre as daybreak

   kindles its fire in the east, and she lights the flame, dives in, and comes up
queen no more, but Narada. "This," says Vishnu, "is *maya's* raj,

   jailer extraordinaire. For whom do you weep, Narada?" This is the "Q"
really in Q&A. For whom do we weep? In dreams we are Richard III,

   ink-stained pen pushers, scullery maids, a hunched-over Laurence Olivier
starring as the evil king on stage, Marilyn Monroe on Harry Cohn's couch.

   Here's to the movie queens with their nose jobs, snow jobs, blow jobs.
"The beauty thing was fun," Ava said later in Madrid walking along,

   gabbing with a friend, passing Pam-Pam's, a local burger joint
under the white sky. "But I'd work at Pam-Pam's before I'd take off

   for Hollywood and star in another crappy movie." O Vishnu,
Vishnu, make me dive into that lake every minute of my misbegotten life,

   every time I forget I am Narada following the black *V*
wild birds make in an autumn sky. Here's to the mosquito, Lord,

   drinking our blood, be we factory worker, star, wife, widow,
X-rated movie actress, saint, burger flipper, barfly, sporadic mechanic,

   clown, or crone. Empty me of everything I am—sphinx, minx,
yogi, yeti, yenta, yodeling nun. Forgive me for being so dense, so numb.

   Break my back with the beauty of the world. Throw me in solitary,
zip me into a shroud. Throw a match on the pyre, rend the veil of *maya*,

   annex me as the Nazis annexed Poland, help me pass your pop quiz.

Ode on Laundry, Lester Young, and Your Last Letter

I'm folding laundry two or three weeks before Christmas,
　　listening to Lester Young's whispering sax embarrass
the afternoon with its lax hold on each note, letting
　　one go, then pulling it back into his bell, strutting
a bit, Mr. Cock-a-doodle-do, and then he soars
　　over sooty buildings like a raven, walls and doors
below like toy houses. You've been dead twelve years, and still
　　I look for you in passing faces—eyes, hands, the trill
of your laughter, but you're gone much as the arpeggio
　　that disappears into Oscar's piano solo
or the black T-shirts under the stacks of boxer shorts
　　and lime green cotton panties, the piling on of hurts,
warts, dirt, and the scraping away. There's my stardust
　　erupting on the other side of the solo. I must
have read your last letter a thousand times, the paper
　　almost transparent. I look at the curve and taper
of your handwriting for a message beyond the words,
　　and between the upslanted lines of *A*'s and *Z*'s I've heard
you promise everything that time has taken back like Billie's
　　wounded voice that's arched and pulling now on the CD
player. I am left here with three mementos—the letter,
　　a photo-booth black-and-white with four frames, a stutter
of time, both of us with long hair, mine blonde, yours as dark
　　as a starless night, laughing at nothing. And there's the scarf
you knitted, full of holes, that I take out every winter
　　and wrap around my neck, touching it as if I were
touching you once last time. So many things have changed. I've cut

my hair, and it has darkened, as the day has. What
if you were sitting with me now, Billie and Lester
    sliding between each other's voices, the register
soaring and dipping like a hunter's bird? What could I say
    that I didn't say? There is only this—the every day
of laundry, this music, the honking trucks on the street
    below, and women with bags rushing home on hurried feet.

9 Sonnets from the Psalms

Hear my prayer, O Lord, though all I do all day is watch
old black-and-white movies on TV. Speak to me
through William Powell or Myrna Loy, solve the mystery
of my sloth. Show me the way to take a walk or catch
a cold, anything but read another exposé
of the Kennedys. Teach me to sing or at least play
the piano. For ten years I took lessons, and all
I learned was to hate Bach. Shake me up or down. Call
me names. Break my ears with AC/DC—I deserve far
worse. Rebuke me in front of my ersatz friends. Who cares?
They don't like me much anyway. Make me fat in lieu
of thin. Give me a break or don't. I'm a hundred million
molecules in search of an author. If that's you, thank you
for my skin. Without it I'd be in worse shape than I'm in.

I beseech thee, O Yellow Pages, help me find a number
for Barbara Stanwyck, because I need a tough broad
in my corner right now. She'll pour me a tumbler
of scotch or gin and tell me to buck up, show me the rod
she has hidden in her lingerie drawer. She has a temper,
yeah, but her laugh could take the wax off a cherry red
Chevy. "Shoot him," she'll say merrily, then scamper
off to screw an insurance company out of another wad
of dough. I'll be left holding the phone or worse, patsy
in another scheme, arrested by Edward G. Robinson
and sent to Sing Sing, while Barb lives like Gatsby
in Thailand or Tahiti, gambling the night away until the sun
rises in the east, because there are some things a girl can be sure
of, like morning coming after night's inconsolable lure.

Some days I feel like Janet Leigh in *Touch of Evil*—
I wake up, sunny and blonde, but by the time midnight
rolls around I've been hijacked by Akim Tamiroff's
greasy thugs, shot up with heroin, framed for murder,
and I'm out cold in a border town jail. I didn't kill
Akim, of course, it was Hank Quinlan—drunk, overweight
Orson Welles—who for thirty-odd years as sheriff
has been framing creeps for crimes they maybe did. Enter
Mike Vargas, tall handsome Mexican cop—Charlton
Heston with a weird little mustache and a dark tan
from a can. "You don't talk like a Mexican," Welles
says, which speaks to me, because I can see how talking
like a Mexican could solve any number of roadside hells
I am currently running away from—well, walking.

What profit is there in being Marlene Dietrich
if you don't rip the intestines out of some dummkopf
who adores you? Is it DNA, karma, or luck
that puts Moses on the mountain and the golden calf
below with the sinning throng? You are that shining bovine
in goddess form, divine Marlene, though I, of course,
dream only of your outfits—Catherine the Great's ermine
hat; the torn sailor's pants and mannish suits in *Witness*
for the Prosecution; the cowboy vest in *Rancho*
Notorious. For me, Barbie dolls were all about
the clothes. I want a Dietrich doll with the fishnet hose
and top hat from *The Blue Angel*. I want a doll who'll flout
Cossacks, British law, a cellar full of drunk GIs,
a real doll—one who drinks martinis, laughs, talks, and lies.

Examine me, O Lord, for I have loved the trivial,
have turned the pages of magazines so glossy
and insubstantial they almost seem to unravel
before my eyes. Ask me any question you like; see
what I'll say. If I don't know the answer, I'll make up
a lie. Throw me in Hell. I'll probably like it there—
the heat, the company, the backbiting badinage. Step
up to the plate, and see if you can make me care
like killer Jimmy Cagney in *White Heat* after he
hears his mother's dead. Screaming, he runs down a table
in the prison dining room, over tin plates of peas,
meat loaf, and glasses of milk. I'd like to be able
to break out of prison just once, steal a car, head
for Mexico, fill my own two-timing brain with lead.

I will praise you, Constance Bennett, for all the great lines
you had in *Topper,* beginning with, "You know something,
George? I think we're dead." Haven't we all felt that from time
to time—dead, I mean—bloodless and out of it, humming
a few bars of "Pink Cadillac" to cheer ourselves up,
though usually it takes something more to shake Virgil
and climb out of hell? I, for one, prefer a hard slap
on the kisser, but Bogart's dead and George Raft, too. Still,
Bela Lugosi might do. No, being a vampire
has nothing to do with being dead. I've done some
unpleasant things in my time: eating brains, changing a tire,
the usual sex stuff with men I didn't like. "Come
hell or high water," my mother used to say when I
had to scrub the world's toilets. Mom, you didn't lie.

The fool hath said in his heart, There is no God. I am
that Trinculo, wandering this blue-green island, drunk
in the company of clowns, waiting for a telegram
that will boost me out of my present jam. Oh, yes ma'am,
I'm in quicksand and thinking about *The Mummy* sunk
under a 4,000-year curse, or is it Caliban
skulking in the underbrush of my mind? What's this funk
that's grabbed me like a gorilla in love? If I can
shake-and-bake it into the next century, slam dunk
it into a FedEx box, send it to Kalamazoo,
then maybe I'll be able to breathe, but that low-down skunk,
my heart, won't quit beating for Prospero and his stew
of thunder and magic, so I stay up nights and scour
the sky for Zeus, his bolts shaking the midnight hour.

Plead my cause, Max von Sydow, because you look like God
more than most men, and because you outfoxed the devil
in one of those rip-your-heart-out Bergman films that made
my twenties so hard to bear. After *The Seventh Seal*,
getting married and buying a house seemed pretty pointless,
though I managed to overcome my reluctance, sex
being the motivating factor in that dilemma, a quick caress
more potent than any job, the deep jungle hex
that leaves you panting for more. So you see, my dear Max,
why I need a divine attorney, and not Mary,
because women do not go for my BS. Here are the facts:
my looks have skedaddled, I don't have a dime, I turn fifty-
one tomorrow. I await celestial pipe and drums,
though why, I have no idea. I'll take whatever comes.

My soul cleaveth unto such trash, a Bombay landfill
could not hold it all. My horoscope in a supermarket
tabloid says, Sunday I'll work my magic on some heart,
but by Friday a storm will blow in from Galveston, steal
my beau, and mow the roof right off my house. I hate vain
thoughts, but what else do I have? Lose ten pounds in two days.
I'm sure amputation can solve some problems. Who's to say?
I take an online test and find I am a mastermind,
plotting world domination from my kitty-cat spot
in front of the TV where I'm watching Garbo rant
and drink champagne. She has amnesia, and Eric von Stroheim's
her boyfriend. He's been my boyfriend, too, and I've sought
solace in a glass, bubbles crowding my scattershot
brain, its stutter like an engine warming up in the rain.

A Birdman to You, Baby

An acrobat in the circus—he was a teenager, a trapeze whiz
    zigzagging across the big top in a skin-tight lavalava.
Burt Lancaster, a real star, from *The Killers* to *1900* to *Atlantic City*,
    yearning for a beautiful broad. He's sometimes big and dumb,
conned by Ava Gardner, but what man could withstand her hex,
    extravagant décolleté, siren song in a black dress, a kind of tantric
doom in the form a mobster's moll, heart like a piece of hollow
    wood. Poor Burt takes the rap for her, those damned marigold
eyes, and goes from packing a rod to wielding a homemade shiv,
    Valentino of the yardbirds. Oh, Burt, Ava took you for a ride,
femme, angel, buttercup, frail. It had nothing to do with you.
    Under the mattress of that princess was a pea so bitter that if
God were still flinging his mojo around the proverbial juke joint,
    then she might be scrubbing floors, but I'm a deist at heart, bootleg
hacker into divine systems of art and death. Who says Shiva's
    so bad? The Destroyer—now there's a moniker to psych
idiots into giving up their grain. Shiva has some experience with fear,
    raising a ruckus, kicking the shit out of everyone. This morning, I
jump through the hoops of the daily news; everything's Iraq, Iraq, Iraq,
    quick stop on a juggernaut through the Middle East, our hajj,
kleptomaniac once-in-a-lifetime trip to the oil Mecca. Here's the poop,
    Pop, everyone's watching the war as if it were *Maverick*, network
lapdogs frowning as if they were real human beings, only so-so
    on the verisimilitude, reporting a final shootout at the OK Corral.
Man, I hate the circus. Those miserable, suffering animals, ratty lion
    numb on downers, snarling at the singing whip. Then wham,
nobody's ready when the lion eats the lion tamer like an Easter ham.

My mom tells this story about a smart boy from her little town
on the Kentucky-Ohio border, son of the high school principal,
    local hero, who turned to robbing banks, killed a cop, small-town bravo,
punkus americanus, but as soon as they'd throw him in the clink
    killer-boy would break out, rob another bank, so he ended up
Quetzalcoatl with clipped wings, in Alcatraz, cellblock 46-J,
    jailbird for life, because no one breaks out of there, even if his IQ
rates up there with Einstein's—wild-haired quantum swami
    in sheep's clothing. So this two-bit genius bank robber
starts swimming, tearing through the icy water like some kind of fish.
    He almost makes it, too, but they drag his cop-killing felonious
tookus back to the rock, where he dies, I guess, an old thug
    gone to seed, like a bad translation of the Icarus myth—wings, flight,
underwater grave, grieving father, mother killing herself.
    Frailty, thy name is human. Oh, Hamlet, your dad is dead, and you
very well may be, too, because sometimes for fun, Death dresses up as life,
    even faking a heartbeat, sitting down in front of the satellite TV
with a double martini and bowl of Doritos. But he'll always be dead,
    Dr. Death, though, of course, his dog still loves him, bow-wow,
except he's watching TV, too, a movie in which a drooling maniac
    chases a blonde with a D-cup through post-nuclear Phoenix.
You may not be dead, but you know what it's like to be *The Blob*.
    Burt's on channel 52, ruffling a sparrow's feathers, its downy
zebra-striped head—Daedalus sending his boy into wide-screen Cinerama
    America, where we're all busting our asses trying to break into Alcatraz.

Ode to Airheads, Hairdos, Trains to and from Paris

For an hour on the train from Beauvais to Paris
    Nord I'm entertained by the conversation of three
American girls about their appointment the next
    day with a hairdresser, and if there is a subtext
to this talk, I'm missing it, though little else. Will bangs
    make them look too dykey? And layers, sometimes they hang
like the fur of a shaggy dog. Streaks, what about blond
    streaks? "Whore," they scream, laughing like a coven of wild
parrots, and after they have exhausted the present
    tense, they go on to the remembrance of hairdos past—
high school proms, botched perms, late-night drunken cuts. The Loch Ness
    Monster would be lost in their brains as in a vast, starless
sea, but they're happy, will marry, overpopulate
    the earth, which you can't say about many poets,
I think a few weeks later taking the 84
    bus to the hairdresser, where I'll spend three long hours
and leave with one of the best cuts of my life from Guy,
    who has a scar on his right cheek and is Israeli,
but before that I pass a hotel with a plaque—
    Attila József, great Hungarian poet, black
moods and penniless, lived there ten years before he threw
    himself under a train in Budapest. If we knew
what the years held, would we alter our choices, take the train
    at three-twenty instead of noon, walk in the rain
instead of taking the Métro? The time-travel films
    I adore speak to this very question: overwhelmed
by disease and war, the future sends Bruce Willis back

to stop a madman. I could be waiting by the track
as József arrives in Paris, not with love but money,
    which seemed to be the missing ingredient, the honey
he needed to sweeten his tea. Most days I take the B
    line of the RER, and one of the stops is Drancy,
the way station for Jews rounded up by the Nazis
    before being sent in trains to the camps, but we can't see
those black-and-white figures in the Technicolor
    present like ghosts reminding us with their pallor
how dearly our circus of reds and golds has been purchased
    and how in an instant all those colors could be erased.

Mambo Cadillac

Drive me to the edge in your Mambo Cadillac,
    turn left at the graveyard and gas that baby, the black
night ringing with its holy roller scream. I'll clock
    you on the highway at three a.m., brother, amen, smack
the road as hard as we can, because I'm gonna crack
    the world in two, make a hoodoo soup with chicken necks,
a gumbo with a plutonium roux, a little snack
    before the dirt-and-jalapeño stew that will shuck
the skin right off your slinky hips, Mr. I'm-not-stuck
    in-a-middle-class-prison-with-someone-I-hate sack
of blues. Put on your high-wire shoes, Mr. Right, and stick
    with me. I'm going nowhere fast, the burlesque
queen of this dim scene, I want to feel the wind, the Glock
    in my mouth, going south, down-by-the-riverside shock
of the view. Take me to Shingles Fried Chicken Shack
    in your Mambo Cadillac. I was gone, but I'm back
for good this time. I've taken a shine to daylight. Crank
    up that radio, baby, put on some dance music
and shake your moneymaker, doll, rev it up to Mach
2, I'm talking to you, Mr. Magoo. Sit up, check
out that blonde with the leopard print tattoo. O she'll lick
    the sugar right off your doughnut and bill you, too, speak
French while she do the do. *Parlez-vous français?* So, pick
    me up tonight at ten in your Mambo Cadillac
cause we got a date with the devil, so fill the tank
    with high-octane rhythm and blues, sugarcane, and shark
bait, too. We got some miles to cover, me and you, think

Chile, Argentina, Peru. Take some time off work;
we're gonna be gone a lot longer than a week
    or two. Is this D-day or Waterloo? White or black—
it's up to you. We'll be in Mexico tonight. Pack
    a razor, pack some glue. Things fall apart off the track,
and that's where we'll be, baby, in our Mambo Cadillac,
    cause you're looking for love, but I'm looking for a wreck.

O'ahu Mambo

Make me a bowl of saimin like *da kine* at Shiro's
    in Pearl City or Palace on North King, the *ono*
kine, cause I'm in the Mainland, and I don't want ramen
    but the big thing, noodles and broth that tastes like the ocean
with fish cake, bok choy, barbecue pork, a little green
    onion and maybe some Spam. Oh, man, you *nevah* seen
anything like it. Make me a plate lunch, daddy, one scoop macaroni
    salad, two scoop rice, and chicken katsu or lomi
salmon. I want some poke, lau lau, kalua pig
    washed down with guava nectar or Primo and a big
shave ice for dessert with mango or lilikoi. Take
    me to the LikeLike Drive-in, L & L, make
a circuit of the island, Waipahu, Waialae,
    Haleiwa, Laie. Take me home to Waianae,
1962, little pink house on Puhano
    Street with a guava tree in the backyard, radio
playing Nat King Cole while we're ironing shirts. O Clara,
    load up the kids in your blue Peugeot. Makaha
beckons, the Coronet store with bolts of blue and white
    polished cotton. Make us muumuus and aloha shirts,
Mama, on your black Singer sewing machine, line us
    up for Sunday School at Waianae Baptist, Jesus
be praised and pass the *li hing mui*, shredded mango, dried
    squid after swimming in Pokai Bay, *haole* skin fried
till we're brown as baked beans, hair white as clouds in the sky,
    Mt. Ka'ala like a green god sleeping on the dry
leeward side of the island. I'm begging you, Kū,

god of war, whipping up fire in my brain, and you
Pele, red-eyed goddess of the sleepless night: take me

back to Leonard's on Kapahulu, all the aunties
lined up for *malasadas* soft as their arms. Open

the stores that closed when I was in the Mainland, when
I was growing twenty-nine plumerias in pots

just for the broken smell in a rainstorm. Give me hot
days at Waimanalo, Arakawa's crammed aisles, let

me eat steaming bowls of noodles till I can eat
no more, drinking the broth as a dying woman drinks

in her last piece of the day, because I'm on the dark
ledge of the Pali, jumping into the wind-whipped sky,

aloha nui loa, my mouth filled with goodbye.

Lingo Sonnets

With twenty-six soldiers I conquered the world.

Johannes Gutenberg

Aloha, Dad, Au Revoir, Goodbye

All the mockingbirds in the world are in a hubbub,
chittering, abuzz, because a good-looking man is dead,
Elvis drawl drawing up inside his flat cocoon, not a little deaf.
Gone is the slim boy in the Philippines after the war, rich
is the red clay of Hawai'i with all his names: Tom, Tommy, T. J.,
kahuna of the sad story, Machiavelli of the slow twist, local
Macbeth of his own days. Would that heaven could open
on him like God's purse and gold pour out its mighty pomp,
quell the roar of his Jerusalem. Amp up your stellar radar,
sir, because you are taking off for worlds unknown, this your rocket
ushering in a new age, because every sap from Tennessee to Tel Aviv
worships at your matchbook shrine. Shake off that ancient jinx,
you mumble-führer, O Daddy O king of the coffee shop kibbitz.

Betty Boop's Bebop

Because I'm a cartoon airhead, people think it's a picnic
down on these mean streets. Sure, my skirt's short, but it's a crime,
fellows, how you give a frail the slip, leave her simmering,
hot and bothered. I have feelings, cardboard, but bordering on ennui,
just this side of tristesse. I may not be human, but I can kick
like one and bite and pinch, too. Don't forget, mister, I'm
not just a bimbo with a helium voice. I'm no rococo
parvenu pillhead. I've read your Rilke, your Montesquieu.
Really, I'm not as dumb as I look. Or maybe I am. Less
tries to be more, but ends up being nothing. My last beau
vetoed the philosophy of religion class in favor of pre-law,
exactly why I don't know, but I'm getting a glimmer. Stay
zany, the cartoonists tell me, and next year you'll play Cinderella.

Caliban Passes His Driving Test on the Ninth Try

Can I tell you a secret? Parallel parking was nothing. I could
even fake the hand signals most of the time—well, maybe half.
Going straight was my bête noir. Give me a freeway and crash!
I was driving back from a gambling weekend in Atlantic City, N.J,
keister strapped tight, following all the rules, when the wheel
made a mad dash for freedom. I can drive any road on any mountain,
only one hand, but a straightaway turns me into Mr. Twitchy. Keep
quiet about it, will ya? I'm trying to get a chauffeur's license. Four
sevens and I took home twenty grand. I gave the cop a ten spot
under the neon 7-Eleven sign near exit 282. The *E* and *V*
were on the blink, sputtering like Prospero when his little minx
yelled *Rape*. All I wanted from the drip was a simple waltz
around the campsite, a kiss. Sheesh—women! Hey, watch that curb!

Desdemona Resuscitated by Sir John Falstaff, EMT

Doppelganger or damsel in distress, it was all one to me
from the first time I checked her lily-white pulse—heading
horizontal. So I figure I'll try the breath of life. Gadzooks! I
just made it, her chest rising hard as a horse's kick,
like a battlefield cannon. Don't get me wrong. I'm
no miracle worker, but I know a thing or two about pulses, so
press the chest hard—the heart is buried deep. You can't rescue
Rapunzel from the tower with a limp handshake. As
the blood starts pumping, you see it in the cheeks first. You
vow to drink less every time you lose one, then drink more. Wow,
X-rays are crazy, man. Last week a guy swallowed a gas cap. Why?
Zounds! Who knows? Maybe he had a slow leak inside, a
butane fire in his gut. Zeus! That could make a snowman panic.

Elizabeth Cady Stanton Writes the Dictionary

Even Susan thought I was too radical by half,
giving women the right to sue for divorce. Hush,
I said, it will all be ours one day. A beautiful (adj.)
knife, the mind, cutting through that Victorian drivel.
My brain and Susan's voice—we were an army (noun)
of two with thousands of foot soldiers. The backdrop
(q.v.) was the (art.) civil war, emancipation, and after
slaves were free, why not women? Marching got
us nothing, but black men got the vote. Universally (adv.)
we were screwed. Susan got back on her soapbox,
yelling about the vote, her one-note harangue. Chintz
armchairs were not for her, Quaker virago moving (verb)
countries into a time they could not, but for her, yet behold.

Friday Slams Crusoe

For Christ's sake, he was a bum. If only I'd written the sodding
history of our stinking stay on that godforsaken island, because I
juggled all the work while he lazed around like a lizard and took
long naps or read under the palms. "Teach me," I begged him,
not that he could be bothered at first. He had a Bible but with no
Psalms or Proverbs. All he'd talk about was Jonah, his rescue,
rereading the passage until finally I could make out words,
teaching myself the rest. I still can't believe how Jacob tricked Esau,
viper in a brother's clothing. You white men throw a shadow
exactly where you want it to fall, sun be damned. I'll say
zed about the sleeping arrangements in our hut. That's a
biblical story of another kind, like London's Babel of street music,
damned water surrounding everything again as far as I can see.

Ganymede's Dream of Rosalind

Girlfriend, I am the boyfriend you never had—honeysuckle mouth,
indigent eyes, no rough Barbary beard when kissing me. Popinjay,
keep me in your little chest, nestle me in your cosy love hotel,
my mouthful of tangy violets, my pumpkin raviolo, my spoon
of crushed moonlight in June. On your breast let me sup,
quaff the nectar of your sweet quim, trim repository of dear
succulence. Only touch my cheek with your hand, and let
us again meet as we did that first time in Act II, Scene IV
when we ran away to the Forest of Arden. Rough sphinx,
you know my heart, because it's yours, too, and quartz,
altogether transparent stone. I yearn for you as a crab
craves the wet sand, a wildebeest the vast savannah, a toad
every mudhole and mossy shelf. Forget Orlando. I'll marry myself.

Hope Revived: The Road to Baghdad

Hope here, alive again, exhumed for a USO show, and I
just can't wait to get on the road again. Don't start, I can yack
like nobody's business, but this *meshuga* Saddam—
no one's going to miss him and his gang of torturers. No
point crying over spilt blood, here we are in Iraq
rah, rah with 25 semi-beautiful starlets, some who can sing. So here's
the deal, the desert's dry and the girls need Vaseline. You
vampires can see they're like prunes. They didn't know
exactly what they were getting into here. "120°! Jesus, Bob," they say,
"zip me up but give me a glass of water. I can't sing 'Georgia'
bone dry." Everyone's complaining—the band, the *schvartze* comic.
Don Rickles, now there was a trooper. We'll be in Nineveh, let's see,
Friday unless we're bombed. I've been dead. I'm telling you, it's nothing.

I Find an Entrance to Hell

I'm with my mother in the Social Security office in Honolulu, and Karen J.
Kapenski is sitting across the desk telling this 80-year-old woman she'll
make no money from my father's death, like she lived in that prison
over fifty years for a check every month, and worse than that particular poop,
Queen Karen reveals Ronald Reagan is responsible, which is a bugger
since Mom voted for him both times. On the wall is a portrait of the current
undersecretary of Satan and his grand vizier, a skinny bully and his heavy,
with vice-Satan's head sunk into his chest like melted beeswax,
Young Worthless with his simp's smirk, and I think, What a phiz,
and I know she's going to vote for them again. There's a proverb,
cheesy but apropos, lurking in here somewhere, but I'm as dead as my dad,
easygoing deacon & ladies' man who never thought of anyone but himself.
"God has him now," Mom says, but here are the numbers. You do the math.

Jane Austen Rewrites *Hamlet* with Interruptions
by Russian Poets

Just when I thought it couldn't get any worse, that hack
Lermontov starts with the insults and pistols, and I think I'm
never going to stop him from shooting Ophelia, too witty till that bozo
Pushkin takes over my pen, turns her into a slut, the queue
running down the stairs implacable as *le général janvier*. Mayakovski's
take on the prince is feverish to say the least. *Mon Dieu,*
votre slave, &c. What is it with these Russians? The crow
exists only as a symbol of Hamlet's death. I think not. I'd give my
zinnias and cabbages for a clear head. Tvetsaeva and Akhmatova
barge in from time to time, the former drunk, the later tragic.
Damned Mandelstam has infected my prince. "Razbliuto," he says, "the
feeling you have for one you once loved but love no more." Dig
his grave with an ice pick, which sounds like Stalin, but alas, *c'est moi.*

Karen, David, and I Stop across the Street
from the Pitti Palace

In questi pressi fra il 1868 e il 1869 Fedor Mihailovic Dostoevskij compì il romanzo L'Idiota

Knocking around after dinner at Alla Vecchia Bettola in the cool
Mediterranean evening, we are joined by Prince Myshkin,
of all people, because a plaque above a little paper shop
(quoted in the epigraph of this poem) tells us he was created here, or
so it says. Writers are such liars, and I should know. Fact:
until this moment I'd forgotten about the prince. It's like the TV
Western you watched with such rapture as a kid while eating a bowl of Trix;
you see a raccoon and suddenly remember the Lone Ranger's mask. Jeez,
and I loved Tonto. *Heigh-Ho, Silver*, I'm such a stale piece of crumb
cake, because during the dark night of 1974, Myshkin held my hand,
even though I was more like a shipwreck than a woman—mute, deaf,
gnawing on my own heart as if it were meat, your words a match
I lit to find this place—forever in your debt, Fedor Mihailovic Dostoevskij.

Lysistrata Lectures the Gods

Listen, we're sick of the death counts in the newspaper. I'm
not kidding—this war is crazy. Why can't you give Apollo
prime time? You know—music, art. Any idiot with an IQ
remotely close to that of a tree stump knows wars
tend to solve nothing. I expected more from the gods. You,
Venus, what about love? Or Athena, what can a widow
expect from you? Wisdom doesn't feed the kids. I must say,
Zeus, you're a man, and I know what's on your agenda,
bragging about Leda and throwing thunderbolts, classic
dunderhead behavior. Well, we're in hell, and like Persephone
fighting dark Hades, it's a waste of time. A soldier missing
her arm is going to be missing it forever, ditto a leg. I
just think there's a better way. Mars, are you listening, you jerk?

Mr. Nollie Hinton Talks to Me while
I Test-Drive His 1955 Studebaker

My daddy was a son of a gun, told me that no woman
ought to wear the pants in a family—straight from the Bible. Pop
quoted the Bible a lot, Jeremiah this, Deuteronomy that, or
Second Corinthians. *Don't believe no sticky-pawed politicians that*
underestimate the cunning of the common man, he'd say. Scurvy
words pour out of their mouths like honey, and words can jinx
you like nobody's business. You like this car, I can tell. It'll whiz
across town in a flash. You like barbecue, that's the place. A good rib
can set you right. Best in Callahan, Florida. Push on the clutch and
ease it into fourth. I'm asking fifteen but I'll take thirteen-five. Ask yourself,
go on, if you can afford to say no. It'll be gone by next month.
I have the sweetest wife in the world. We got this car in Canton, N.J.
Keep your foot on the gas, now. You want it, give me a call.

Nietzsche Explains the Übermensch to Lois Lane

No, no, no, no—he doesn't even have nerves of steel. No
point asking him to save you, ma'am, he's more likely to rescue
rain from the street. Born on your block, not Krypton, he's
terror with a capital *T*, the beautiful mind you
vain dames can't see for the mascara on your lashes. You saw
exactly nothing when you clapped eyes on him, a nerdy
zip, not even head of the class, just skulking in the back, a
brilliant light in a room full of blind men. But when he rises, havoc
descends on the world, lightning storms blister the earth, for he
fears nothing, feels nothing, sees everything. From the beginning
he's been a juggernaut, crushing everything in his path, from the Hindi
Jagannath, Lord of the World, a guise of the god Vishnu. A dark
Lex Luthor was more what I was thinking than Superman, ma'am.

Olive Oyl Thinks about Quantum Theory

Oh, I can hear you laughing now. That permanent postnasal drip,
Queen of Saturday Morning—what can she know about math or
science? You'd be surprised. I got straight As when I was at
Ubu Roi High School and Regional Dada Institute. My friend, Bev,
went to raves, smoked pot on the corner. Not me. Forget about sex.
You can guess the kind of guys a skinny gal attracts. Buzz
Abercrombie was my lab partner. We built an atomic bomb,
can you believe it, for our senior project. Our teacher plotzed,
even though it was just on paper, and I did more than my half,
going to the lab every weekend from October until March.
I had a ball at the prom. The music was funky, the DJ
kept playing "Shotgun" by Junior Walker over and over until
midnight. I danced till I disappeared, or so it's seemed since then.

Punk Puck or Robin Goodfellow with Fender Stratocaster

Pass me the beer and the goddamned pool cue,
Romeo. I know, I know, it's
the wrong play but the right place. You
valiant guys get on my nerves. The show
exists only for the tickets—you know, money—
zeroes, and lots of them after a number. I'm a
big guitar now, plowing my supersonic
decibels into the stratosphere,
far away from this soup kitchen of a planet, banging
hymns of anarchy into the universal din. I
jest, of course, the old Puck leaks through the black
light. Bootlicking's my specialty. Was that Coriolanus? I'm
never in the right play. Romeo, wherefore art thou, daddy-o?

Queen Mab Blues

or

Quick, Run for Cover, She's Reading Horace Again

After all these years, Venus, why pick on me?—glib
countess of the last word, queen of the bees. I'm dead,
everyone knows that, breasts sinking, life half
gone—if I'm lucky. I'm praying for cancer, which
is insane, or maybe not. Who's ever ready for that blue jay?
Kiss off, leave me to my books, my pen, my lumps of coal,
my short walks off long piers, *pranayama* for these worn-
out rags of lungs. Quit playing me like a tricked-up pimp
quoting Mercutio: "I see Queen Mab hath been with thee." Rather
shall I say, Shove it all—your quick glances, short
unruly breaths, thumping brain. My heart's a wonky TV
waiting to be turned off. I'm through with you, your hex,
your hungry eyes, mouth, arms, your *ne plus ultra* divine buzz.

Raskolnikov Rates the Plays

Right off the bat, I hate the cross-dressing comedies
the most. There's nothing funny about life on earth, as you
very well know. Let's start with the pawnbroker's brow—
X marks the spot where my ax smashed her head, a wavy
zigzag of blood staining the floor. There's nothing a
boy loves more than mayhem. *Titus*—now there's a comic
dish to set before the king. Or *Richard III*. My God, he
fought like a Cossack. Part monster, part bulldog;
he took the Plantagenets down with him. Of course, I
just adore *Macbeth*, but forget that mealymouthed *Hamlet*—book-
loving malcontent. Give me a tyrant any day—Saddam,
Nebuchadnezzar, both king and bottle of champagne. O
pop a cork for Babylonia—now, I believe, called Iraq.

So Says Cleopatra, Reincarnated as a Hippie Chick, circa 1967

Snakes, snakes, snakes, Ptolemy and Caesar—I ask you, what
ubiquitous black hole was I born under? On TV
Walter Cronkite drones on about the war, but I know it's a tax
you have to pay for being alive. News is just buzz,
a boat of lies launched in a sea of misinformation, Horab
constructing his bridge over the whole fiery sea, and I'd
even bet that particular monster would turn into a wolf
given the right aspect of the moon. However, I'd stake my girlish
intuition that the world is changing. Have some baba ghanouj,
kale casserole, muesli. In fifty years, everyone will be eating a lentil
mess on brown rice, but no one will be hungry. *Dream on,*
O Flower Child, says Set, Bulldog of Death. *Dream on, Lollipop,*
Queen of the Nile. In war Set will ever out-seize her Caesar.

Titus Woos Titania

Tight ass, I like that in a woman. Fairy queen, could you
vamp it up a little, show some more T & A? Screw
ecstasy, I want to show you what pain is. I play a doozy
zero-sum game in the bedroom and in the arena,
because there are plenty more where you came from—chic
ditzes with bleached blonde hair and nipple rings. *She
fools no one who fools herself.* Who said that—Voltaire? Going
home with me will always be an adventure. Remember, I
jilt a girl who doesn't hit back. Was he a hunchback,
le philosophe, or was that Alexander Pope? I'm
not up on your literary chitchat, but I do know a thing or two
pertaining to lust. When I put my hand here, that's your cue—
raise your skirt, fairy queen, and spread those fairy legs.

Ulysses Talks with Freud about the Underworld

Underarm is more like it. In *The Odyssey*, Book V,
when Athena wheedles Zeus into sending Hermes to coax
yummy Calypso into letting me go, I thought, Ulysses, you putz,
all is well. You'll be turning Penelope's doorknob
come not too many moons. I can't remember now how I ended
entering the portals of the Underworld. Ask Homer. If
getting into trouble were box office, I'd be boffo. Hah,
I might as well have my own show. I'd say to Leno, "Jay,
kiss your time slot good-bye." Hell—Achilles was a ghoul,
Mother a breath of sulfur. What does it all mean,
O mein Herr Docktor? Was it all a dream? When I sleep,
quick images flicker across my closed eyes; I hear
saws, smell newly cut wood, and don't give me that Oedipal shit.

Venus and Dogsbody, a Match Made in New Jersey

Venus, you are a major babe. Your hair is way big, and wow,
X-ray glasses are not needed with that see-through foxy
zebra-print chiffon bra and matching thong. Fucking-A
beautiful, I am not like that pansy Adonis. I want a bionic
diva in my king-sized vibrating bed. Come on over here,
fair maid. Ain't that the way youse guys talk? Thanksgiving,
Halloween, Christmas—every day's a holiday with you. I
just can't believe I could get a goddess in the sack.
Let's toot a few lines tonight, my little summer plum,
nip out for a juicy steak in my new candy-flake Eldorado,
play footsie under the table. No Miller High Life and barbecue
ribs for you, baby. Only the best. Put on your high-heel sneakers,
tootsie, because I'm a Sherman tank with guns blazing for you.

Whatever

or

As You Like It, Part Two

While the alcoholic department chair is squeezing your thorax,
you remember the answer to number eleven on the quiz
about Egypt you took in the fifth grade. The word *scarab*
comes to mind, and that's what he looks like—a desiccated
entomological specimen carved in stone. You think, what if
God ended the world at this very moment? Frozen, the breath
in your throat is like an elephant in the herd of a grand maharaj
killed one morning by a freak tornado from Borneo or Nepal.
Miss Harriet Nichiguchi was your teacher, but that was long ago on
O'ahu, and he's not really strangling you, but it feels like it. Pop
quiz—why are you sitting there anyway? Think of the million other
stupid things you could be doing: shopping for dust, perfecting that
ulcer, watching Joan Crawford's kabuki mask crack on TV.

Xerox My Heart, Three-Headed Dog

Xerox my heart, three-headed dog, and send a facsimile copy,
zip code 60606, to Mr. Doesn't-Give-a-Fig-bout-a-
Bloody-Thing. How to describe him—Talmudic, pandemic,
demonic, or all of the demented above? Oh, what did I see,
for God's sake, in him? Was it the totalitarian nickel-squeezing,
his Nazi exercise program for everyone but himself? I must say I
just adored his picking through egg rolls looking for shrimp and pork,
loved his plan for me to go to law school so I could support him.
Nightmares are never over; they roll around in your brain, like Jell-O
primed with exploding fruit. "Rescue me," sings Fontella Bass. Rescue,
reboot, and reinstate me in the human race, because this girl is
taking a taxi to the airport for a jet plane to Paris, France. *Mon Dieu,*
vegan tyrant, this is one cow town I am more than ready to blow.

Yorick's Soliloquy

You could have mentioned me a thousand times, your big schnozz
always in somebody else's business, but it wasn't until the catacomb
crew dug me up that you remembered your old friend who died
either of pneumonia or syphilis. My skull's thin as a leaf,
grim as the jokes that made you laugh like a horse. Though
I was your father's fool, you were my pet, my little jay
kept in a cage only earth can break open. Flesh is halting frail,
meine kleine friend, and your father wasn't such a paragon.
Ophelia makes a pretty corpse, though blood did give her ladyship
quelque choses. I learned my French from *jolie* Mlle. Mercier,
she of the long, red hair, your governess. You didn't know that
unless you were skulking somewhere. So I didn't show up until Act V.
Well, I still made a splash. I don't miss life much—just sex and Bordeaux.

Zeus, It's Your Leda, Sweetie Pie

Zip up your toga, thunder thighs, that's Hera
barking like Cerberus on amphetamines. I was a skeptic,
don't you know, but you've got the equipment, as the
frigging king of the gods should. All the mortal gals are agog,
hinting for an invite to our next divine date, as if I
jump in your Caddy and we race toward a three-star snack,
lightning bolts setting the highway ablaze miles ahead. I'm
nervous about your wife. She blinded Tiresias, and Apollo
plays possum when she's around. Zeus, that's your cue—
reassure me. Don't think I want to move to Mt. Olympus.
Those relics are a snooze. Athena, there's dust on her tutu,
Venus's, too, so get a move on, or my Helen will wow
exactly no one and his horse. Let's dillydally, Ding-Dong Daddy.

Don't look for heaven, my heart,
but wear out the pavement of your street.

Pindar,
Pythian Odes, III.61–62

All-Night Lingo Tango

All night I watch the worst movies—musicals of the Nazi blitz,
    Zapruder films of my own assassination, the armada
battles between the hideous face of my Aunt Priscilla and my
    young, beautiful mother, my bit part—sliding from the womb,
coming out, infant debutante, the radio my own personal haruspex
    exorcising future devils hovering in the hospital room, out-of-sync
disaster lodged in my baby-soft skull like a stuttering misanthropic crow,
    wild with rockabilly delusions of the coming years. Old
Everyman, Hamlet, says something apropos at the end of Act V:
    "Venom, to thy work." Claudius and everyone else is out of time,
for the news is always bad or haven't you noticed? *Mon Dieu,*
    underestimate me, and you'll be right on the money. *Woof, woof*
goes the lycanthropic late-night host or as sez dapper ghost Cary Grant,
    Topper, here we are at the Kirby kennel, barking,
howling, and biting permissible. Biting a hunk from someone's ass
    seems so beautiful right now in my room at the Hate Hotel, which
is right next door to the Insomnia Inn. All I need is a ten-hour stupor,
    ripe with Technicolor dreams to turn me into Saint Francis, but as I
jump into a James Bond scene, I am blown to smithereens. Where's my Q,
    quick-draw disseminator of hidden weapons, because there's O. J.
kicking up the dirt? "Kiss off, haole girl," he says, snapping his whip.
    Perhaps this is the end? No such luck, because as everyone knows luck
loves a loser, and miraculously reconstituted I ski off down the slopes—*No-o-*
    o-o-o. That scene didn't last long. They rarely do at the No-tell Motel
my dreams shack up in or the double-wide trailers of my nightmares. In
    no time I'm back on a train hurtling though Bavaria, Herr Mayhem
nodding his crew-cut head on my shoulder, drooling on my silk blouse. I'm

Miss Popularity tonight. Everyone wants to be my friend, even
Orson Welles, sultan of lost sleds, squiring Rita Hayworth around Babel.

Lo, how the mighty have fallen into a vat of boiling oil, into
pots of yummy money, into tubs of KFC. Poor damaged Rita and her swank

kingpin of the long shot. Oh, to fill a dress the way she did, nuclear hip,
quantum belly, legs like your first dream of suicide; reminds me of Sgt. Maj.

John Hodiak flogging the conscripts into a tatterdemalion queue
right under the noses of the Japanese guards or was it German? World War II

invades the Right Bank of my left brain around four a.m. or as Homer
says, when the rosy-red finger of dawn pulls the trigger on another night. Oh,

here's to the poppy and all her dreamy cousins once removed, the bastards,
too, Nyquil and Xanax, true blue in their gondola of swoon—going, going,

gone into last round of the final lap of the first breath, as Juliet
uncurls her fingers from Morpheus's dark form, so do I bodysurf

from Haleiwa to Makapu, searching not for Romeo but Keanu,
vatic messiah of the Underworld, whose undertow has taken me

everywhere I've wanted to go. O Night—thief, crook, ganev
with a heart of iron—deliver me from this your diabolical bed,

descend on me like Hurricane Medusa and her demon peepshow,
exhume me, penetrate my bodice, because I'm locked in your tantric

cage, filled like a bottle of sin, stuffed in your most celestial box,
your map of a hundred thousand dead ends. Dive bomb me, dream sahib,

blast this fortress of din, divide me until I disappear, give me my
Zen canoe, my Theravadan rescue from the burning bush, throw in amnesia,

a poison apple, a knife in the back. My kingdom for a nuclear gin fizz.

Ode on Dictionaries

A-bomb is how it begins with a big bang on page
    one, a calculator of sorts whose centrifuge
begets *bedouin, bamboozle, breakdance,* and *berserk,*
    one of my mother's favorite words, hard knock
clerk of clichés that she is, at the moment *going ape*
    the current rave in the fundamentalist landscape
disguised as her brain, a rococo lexicon
    of Deuteronomy, Job, gossip, spritz, and neocon
ephemera all wrapped up in a pop burrito
    of movie star shenanigans, like a stray Cheeto
found in your pocket the day after you finish the bag,
    tastier than any oyster and champagne fueled *fugue*
gastronomique you have been pursuing in France
    for the past four months. This 82-year-old's rants
have taken their place with the dictionary I bought
    in the fourth grade, with so many gorgeous words I thought
I'd never plumb its depths. Right the first time, little girl,
    yet here I am still at it, trolling for pearls,
Japanese words vying with Bantu in a goulash
    I eat daily, sometimes gagging, sometimes with relish,
kleptomaniac in the candy store of language,
    slipping words in my pockets like a non-smudge
lipstick that smears with the first kiss. I'm the demented
    lady with sixteen cats. Sure, the house stinks, but those damned
mice have skedaddled, though I kind of miss them, their cute
    little faces, the whiskers, those adorable gray suits.
No, all beasts are welcome in my menagerie, ark

of inconsolable barks and meows, sharp-toothed shark,
OED of the deep ocean, sweet compendium
of candy bars—Butterfingers, Mounds, and M&Ms—
packed next to the tripe and gizzards, trim and tackle
of butchers and bakers, the painter's brush and spackle,
quarks and black holes of physicists' theory. I'm building
my own book as a mason makes a wall or a gelding
runs round the track—brick by brick, step by step, word by word,
jonquil by *gerrymander*, *syllabub* by *greensward*,
swordplay by *snapdragon*, a never-ending parade
with clowns and funambulists in my own mouth, homemade
treasure chest of tongue and teeth, the brain's roustabout, rough
unfurler of tents and trapezes, off-the-cuff
unruly troublemaker in the high church museum
of the world. O mouth—boondoggle, auditorium,
viper, gulag, gumbo pot on a steamy August
afternoon—what have you not given me? How I must
wear on you, my Samuel Johnson in a frock coat,
lexicographer of silly thoughts, billy goat,
X-rated pornographic smut factory, scarfer
of snacks, prissy smirker, late-night barfly,
you are the megaphone by which I bewitch the world
or don't as the case may be. O chittering squirrel,
ziplock sandwich bag, sound off, shut up, gather your words
into bouquets, folios, flocks of black and flaming birds.

Ode to Odor, Ardor, and the Queen's Chickabobboo

Harold Pinter is drinking a bottle of champagne
    during intermission at the Cottesloe, the rain
of words ceasing for thirty minutes, so the skein
    of lies Chekhov's characters tell themselves while they feign
desire or perhaps love, drink vodka shots, and complain
    about provincial life can soak into the terrain
of our minds, though how we can possibly regain
    our hold on joy after watching Ivanov's insane
hectoring of his dying wife I can't see. It's plain
    the great playwright feels the same as I watch him drain
glass after glass of so-so theater-bar champagne,
    and I think of a group of nineteenth-century Plains
Indians, visiting Paris and tasting champagne,
    calling it the Queen's chickabobboo, and may she reign
supreme, because nothing can break the dreary membrane
    of November fog like a glass of Veuve Clicquot, vain
thoughts exploding like a silly *Mikado* refrain,
    and even the most jaded, worn out demimondaine
will raise her glass to what? Tomorrow? The last domain
    of hope until it takes its final dip in the Seine,
though there is probably a French heaven of Gitane-
    soaked cafés, populated by Rimbaud and Verlaine,
poetes maudits plus, or, even better, the Great Dane,
    Hamlet, nothing wrong with him that a little champagne
couldn't cure, right, Sir Harold? Or did you choose to remain
    plain Mr. Pinter? Who knows or cares? I entertain
so many idle thoughts that the inner cupcake of my brain

has mounted an armed and, may I say, vicious campaign
against itself and its thousands of questions, mostly inane,
    such as, Why do roses smell like mildew, and in Spain
did the lisping begin with a lisping king? Does Bruce Wayne
    aka Batman have the best costume, and the quatrain,
who would put a poem in box? For Macbeth, that Thane
    of Cawdor thing was a real problem. Oh, where is Jane
Austen when you need her? Nursing a pulsing migraine
    or Francis Bacon shouting over shambles, "Real pain
for my sham friends, champagne for my real friends." It's plain
    that pain's the problem—think of poor rich Citizen Kane
whispering "Rosebud" with his last breath or Chekhov again,
    I must be dying. It's so long since I've drunk champagne.

Ode to Diagramming Sentences
in Eighth-Grade English Class
with Moonlight, Drugs, and Stars

Little map, hardly a neighborhood, your long avenues,
    short streets, cul-de-sacs where nouveau riche parvenu
bumpkins have set up house, mowed luscious meadows and fields
    for swimming pools and tennis courts—what can be revealed
from your blackboard-and-three-hole-notebook caliphate
    in the dark, hormone ridden oubliette of the eighth
grade where poems of unpassable beauty are rendered
    as useless as the broken-down Fords with hanging fenders
lined up on the highway between Panacea
    and Tallahassee, Florida? Cassiopeia
of the teeming mind, O sentence, string of words straining
    for sense in the mad jumble like an addict mainlining
heroin or a child stacking blocks. Mighty troika
    of noun, object, and verb, your great guru Franz Kafka
took the tea party of high Victorian lingo
    into the interrogation room of the Gestapo,
sat in its hard chair like a monk without God to guide
    him with the flickering candle of faith. O hundred-eyed
gorgon of Henry James, who drowned in a Bolshevik
    century of lowbrow Newspeak, advertising flacks'
doubleplusgood soda-pop slogans, one day playing Whist
    and the next roiling in a hodgepodge Sadean tryst
with the buff boy on the billboard. Sentence, dear
    arbiter between truth and fact, lead me to the clear
meaning of moonlight, deliver me from the buzzword

that calls murder collateral damage. Raise your sword,
Achilles of *le mot juste,* stumbling virtuoso,
　　sweet sinner in Dante's inferno. My Caruso,
garden spade, pickpocket, fast-order cook's spatula
　　turning burgers on a hot grill, freight train, Dracula,
whatever your faults, you're a beacon of common sense
　　though you can save no one either in past or present tense.

Ode on My 45s, Insomnia,
and My Poststructuralist Superego

O that life could be a day-and-night dance party
    with ginger ale, gin and tonics, or Bacardi
and Coke—who cares?—as long as the music keeps coming
    like a railroad train without brakes, the engine storming
down the tracks, the conductor's hair flying in the night
    air, like a tornado now, because I might
just take off, Little Richard screaming "Tutti Frutti"
    on my little portable record player, duty
fleeing like an *a-wop-bop-a-loo-bop* bomb on speed,
    and though my drug days are behind me, tonight I need
a fix of funk, because, lights low, "Little Red Corvette"
    will cure any ailment, even the knock-down Tourette's
that attacks at three a.m., super-ego Babette,
    snappy little twat with a French accent, legs, you bet,
in fishnet hose and a skirt up to here, snarling, "Slut,"
    though for emphasis she adds, *putain, salope*. "But, but,
but," I stutter, "I haven't slept with anyone but Dave
    for 25 years." "That's what you think, you bourgeois slave,"
and God knows I can let a detail slip, but you'd think
    I'd remember that, so excuse me while I sink
into a slough of despond so deep I can hear Chinese
    beneath my feet, but hold on—What's that?—It's "Please,
Mr. Postman," and the Marvelettes swing down and grab
    me up, for my rock-and-roll ids, Barbie and Babs,
have pushed back the rug, are doing the twist, drinking Tabs.
    "Forget that French bitch and her zombie hoard. You can stab

us in the back and call us Keith Richards," the girls coo,

and then scream the lyrics of "I Put a Spell on You,"

because they've read Heidegger and Simone de Beauvoir,

too, but it's not going stop them swinging *ce soir*,

dancing in the streets with Martha and the Vandellas

and drinking mai tais with little purple umbrellas,

for they reside in the land of a thousand dances

where Wilson Pickett reigns supreme, while I freelance

at the funk bazaar, because some nights Prince's "Kiss"

is all that stands between me and the darkening abyss,

and my girls are swinging their ponytails with Nadine,

Layla, Gloria, because we heard it through the grapevine

that not much longer will we be here, so let's go, girls,

down to the basement and say hello to the devil,

because his dress is red and trouble is on his mind,

and he's out searching for girls, but what does he find

when he gets to the party, revved up, ready to scare

our pants off—our pants are off and we're not fighting fair,

and who is the devil anyway but some ugly

guy with a goatee and fire coming from his ears. We

say, to hell with you, your minions, too, for there's music

in the air, and the night is shorter than your prick,

Satan, so move along, because we have some dancing

to do, in the streets, under the sheets. I'm not mincing

words here, because I've got three girls in one body. Wait,

that smells like religion, which I can do, especially the hate.

Ode to Fear

Dear friend, how many dark alleys have you kept me from,
    how many bubbling potions, witches' brews with brown foam
have you stopped me from chugging like an over-amped frat
    boy at a keg party on Saturday night, game lost
that afternoon to unranked Clemson while his power-
    house number-one school choked again in double over-
time? Or think of the doors you have locked, the deadbolts turned
    when I was too drunk to walk, talk, but not sing. You churned
inside me like Barry Manilow riding a wave
    at Waimea or Maria Callas as a slave
girl yodeling for her prince or poor Lana Turner,
    her fingerprints all over the gun but her sweater
snug, while the DA struggled to make her admit her

boyfriend hadn't done it alone. Remember the first
    time I had sex? I used three kinds of birth control, wished
I'd had four. Thanks for making it so much fun for me,
    and the boy, too—where did you pick him up? What a spree
that was, though I did rededicate my life to George
    Eliot. How many times must a girl forage
her way through *Middlemarch* before she is free to make
    her own decisions? More than twenty? Why don't we skate
past that one? Ted Bundy was living on the next block,
    so your rules probably saved my hide, and I'm in hock
to you for a hundred thousand "no's" that just tripped off
    my tongue like broken teeth after a fight. I was tough
because of you, though I looked like a powder puff,

all pink and sweet. Thanks for hiding me when the slavers
     were scouring my village, for making me quiver
in the shadows while my girlfriends walked the plank in white
     lace, for making me tremble before every damned flight,
for the Friday and Saturday nights I didn't waste
     at the Pastime chatting up bores. John Keats was my date
and Oscar Wilde and that paranoid hipster Ginsberg,
     who taught me to rant like Job. Thanks for the giant surge
of adrenaline every night before sleep can chew
     a hole in my mind, and while I play peekaboo
with death, you hold my hand. That's sweet, a bit of soft-shoe
     before the ax falls, because we're all living on the Rue
Morgue, so come to mama, you big bad grizzly bear, you.

Ode on Cake, Catcalls, Eggs
with a Minor Scary Reference to the End of the World

A new friend and I stop for drinks, and she becomes crazed
    and says the tapas can't have a drop of mayonnaise
in them because she's a vegan, and since we're in Spain
    and my Spanish is even worse than hers, we explain
in dog-Spanish that she can't eat anything with eggs,
    and the waiter looks as if he'd rather serve Queequeg,
the giant tattooed sailor from *Moby Dick,* than two
    sniffy American señoras with no clue
about chorizo, gambas, or anything tasty,
    and we make no friends for our beleaguered country,
not to mention our age group, which is no longer young,
    and I remember at twenty-two being stung
by catcalls and whistles. How dare they? I fumed, their dog-
    language lost on me, because they were saying, "You're young,
woof woof, pretty," which doesn't seem so bad now that time
    has had his way with me, and our waiter is cute. I'm
on his side. For years I was a vegetarian,
    so I know food hang-ups like a Rastafarian
knows ganja, but I've left self-abnegation behind
    me like a crumpled party dress on the floor or a mind
blown by a cocktail of acid and Jimi Hendrix,
    and as I see it this woman is in a bad fix,
because she hasn't eaten cake in ten years, real cake
    with butter and eggs and whole milk, not those nasty fake
cakes made with apple sauce, oat bran, and whole wheat flour,
    flat as a pancake, which is all they are, like the dour

Scottish oatcake, and *eggs*, what a word, the Anglo Saxon
    eggys, that for some reason trumped the much more common
eyren when English was sorting itself out, madam
    and her lord eating pastries while the farmer ate jam
and cake, because John Wycliffe in his great translation
    of the Bible speaks of a "round kaak of breed," though none
would call bread *cake,* especially her majesty Marie Antoinette,
    but there is *panettone,* the cake Italians eat
at Christmas, which means *big bread*, though it's golden with eggs
    as is every *torta* in Christendom with its figs
and raisins, sugar and chocolate, for we all need cake
    because the world could end at any moment, boom, and make
us little more than dust. My dear friends, I ask you, what
    is life without cake? Bundt, spice, coconut, chocolate?
What about birthdays? Weddings? Funerals? Wakes?
    Who would marry without a three-tiered cake, and I hate
to think of turning eight without a Batman sheet cake,
    so eat up, amigos, because everyone is hungry,
and the earth gives us grain, sugar cane, pecan trees,
    and milk cows the size of SUVs filled to the brim
with what we need to make shortbread, biscuits, cookies, cream
    puffs, so here's to eggs and all the hens who laid them.

Ode to Little Boys

With six nephews and two stepsons, my days have been rich
    with little boys and their gorgeous malapropisms
when learning to speak English—"fwasty" for thirsty, which
    lassoes "frosty" into the equation, the schism
between the Gobi of hot-and-dry and the Arctic
    of cold-and-wet solved in one train crash, not to mention
"grails" for girls, "maz-a-geen" for magazine, and "moo-sick,"
    which my younger stepson, cherubic *putto* Ian
Kirby, would yell from his car seat when the radio
    was not blasting rock and roll loud enough for his
three-year-old tastes, sitting there like the Pillsbury Dough-
    boy rocking out to Warren Zevon, not heard at Miss
Pam's School, bastion of mice and cheese, E-I-E-I-O,

"I'm a Little Teapot" and "The Lord is Good to Me"—
    songs that drove my brother to teach his son Steppenwolf's
"Born to Be Wild," Elliot's lisp making the free-
    for-all biker anthem sound as if an Elmer Fudd-tough-
boys-chapter of Hell's Angels had been founded to rock
    the sing-alongs of America's lascivious
preschoolers, because it was this same four-year-old who cocked
    his head and said to me, "I wish girls had penises,"
and when I asked, "Why?" said, "So I could look at them." *Mais*
    oui, but of course, though when my mother-in-law would say,
"When I was a boy," Will, my older stepson, would spray
    saliva across the room, screaming, "Grandma, no way
you were a boy," the horror in his voice betraying

a cocktail of fear and loathing of which Kierkegaard
        would have been proud, because though science and logic
can deliver us from evil, efforts to retard
        the growth of temptation have stymied philosophic
minds throughout the ages, given the ultra-tasty
        nature of the world, and remember "The Emperor's
New Clothes," for it was a boy who saw through the hasty
        confection of the big guy's a-little-more-than-gossamer
pantaloons, which brings me to Matt, my youngest nephew,
        of whom my mother said when he was born, "his
hair was so white, I thought he was an albino," blue
        eyes scotching that prognostication, the same blue eyes
on me now: "Guess my nickname," he says. I have no clue,

and when I beg him to tell me, he says, "Promise not
        to laugh?" I nod, but when he whispers, "Q-tip," of course I
roar with laughter, and he knows I'm laughing at him not
        with him. I say it sounds like the rapper, which he buys,
and I teach him how to play Minesweeper, so we are
        friends again. This is one of the biggest surprises
of my life, how much I love little boys, their hair
        smelling like dirty cookies, the snot, the disguises
I've concocted at Halloween—Superman, Satan,
        Batman, Mutant Ninja Turtles—I, a girly-girl,
who never climbed a tree in her life. O God the bland
        bohemian hell I lived in, psychedelic whirl
of my twenties, the films of Fassbinder and Bergman

I fumed about before Ian ran into the room
        after a dinner party and yelled with glee, "I'm a
little jack mouse." "Jackass," stage-whispered his brother from

the door, but his stooge was lost on laughter's highway,
reveling in his audience, the Goofy flannel
    pajamas I suppose sucked now into the vortex
of time, and even preschool can be a most brutal
    business, worse than many slashers at the Cineplex,
as when I asked Elliot what his teacher had said
    to him that day, and he answered, "No, no, no, no, no!"
or eight-year-old Henry, who loved his dog and wanted
    to be a vet, but he had to say he didn't know
if it ever could be anything more than a so-so

job: "What are you talking about?" asked my sister. "Mom,
    they're always standing on street corners with signs, 'Vet—Will
Work for Food.'" Boys, I'll tell you language doesn't become
    any less squirrelly as time goes on; in fact the squirrel
quotient balloons, and as Will said to my husband when
    he said he was moving out, "Dad, are you going to seek
your fortune?" Who isn't? And if you're lucky, my friend,
    there's a ten-year-old boy inside you—Huck, Tom, Buckwheat,
Alfalfa, Jack Mouse, Q-tip, even Beaver Cleaver,
    because face it the teacher is always yelling, "No!"
and as we speak the emperor has no clothes, and there
    is no ten-year-old boy on CNN, radio,
Fox News, or ABC to say, "Mister, your ass is bare."

Ode to White Peaches, Pennies,
Planets, and Bijou, the Dog

Last night I dreamed of a long-dead dog, the black-and-white
    mutt of the friend who turned on me, venom and spite
pouring from her mouth as the damned erupt from the mouth
    of Satan in the Florence Baptistry—*and so doth*
the heathen rage, as my mother said when my teenaged
    self ranted over some curfew or hem length, a caged
tiger stalking through that beige cinderblock bungalow,
    my dream to become a hybrid of Edgar Allen Poe
and Jane Austen, so I loathed my mother's collection
    of pithy sayings and biblical admonitions,
such as, *vengeance is mine, sayeth the Lord; vanity*
    vanity, all is vanity; don't come crying to me;
who do you think you are, young lady; I can read you
    like a book; you live in a dream world; I don't give two
cents for what you think, a penny for your thoughts, darling,
    though now a penny's not worth much, so they're thinking
of getting rid of it as they did Pluto—the planet,
    not the Roman god—for no matter how you spin it,
penny or planet, death's a bear, though my erstwhile friend's
    dog seems to be doing okay, and said, "Arf, no hard
feelings," and I said, "Sure," because he was a great dog,
    though his mistress was a major nut, two or three cogs
missing in her cranial machinery, but I
    am not thinking of all that so much as I walk by
the stone and terracotta church of Sant'Ambrogio,
    where old Leonardo's teacher Verrocchio

72

is buried, past the handsome tripe sandwich vendor
       with his silver Flash Gordon shoes, past Cibreo's door
and into the market, where in the heat the scent
       of ripe peaches, yellow and white, calls like a serpent
in the garden, bringing to mind the home movie
       of my husband at two, laughing and running as he
held his mother's hand, his head like a white peach. Your hair
       is white again, my darling, and while I despair
of so many things, the perfume of ripe peaches opens
       inside me like a sultan's palace or your mouth when
you first kissed me, every harsh word I'd ever heard slung
       into space, all the peaches of summer on your tongue.

Ode on the Letter *M*

Midway through the alphabet, you are the tailored seam
    that ties *Adam* to *zephyr, atom* to *uranium,*
sword that takes up a new God, little lamb, turns him
    into a flame-spewing Visigoth, and Byzantium
becomes Constantinople, the new Jerusalem,
    hallelujah, bombs away. Or are you the flim-flam
man working small towns in Mississippi—Troy, Denham,
    Tishomingo, Yazoo City—hawking a serum
that will cure everything—warts, impetigo, ringworm—
    fade wrinkles, spark a wilting libido. Oh, yes, ma'am,
dose your husband, and that rooster will crow again, thrum
    like a well-tuned violin. A masterful scam
it was until the day that pretty little schoolmarm
    purred like a pussycat, locked you in her maximum
security prison with gold rings—aluminum
    siding your new game, the highway nothing but a dream
of freedom, because one letter can change grin to grim,
    plug to plum, slut to slum, a few blankets and wampum
can get you Manhattan, itself once New Amsterdam,
    because sometimes we seem to be a quorum
of idiots on a plague ship in a sea of phlegm
    and fog, rumors of disease flying like crows in the scum
of clouds heavy with hurricanes. Or the bride and groom
    in black and white, God bless their little Vietnam,
here's hoping for years of pound cake and hymns. There's a charm
    in myopia, witness Monet's chrysanthemum,
a blob of pink and blue, his lilies smears of thick cream

on green. I take off my glasses when I can, though I'm
as lost as anyone, searching for the perfect dim sum
    restaurant, locked in my high gothic scriptorium,
scratching for words as rats scratch for cheese—Muenster, Edam,
    Livarot—for there are worlds in worlds—Mozart's requiem
the dark river Figaro sails on or *The Tin Drum*
    spawned by the SS. Who can guess the mysteries that cram
our brains? Not I, said the little black cat. Fie, fie, foe, fum,
    I smell the blood of everyone. Like Robert Mitchum
in *Cape Fear*, the ghouls are out, ripping the flesh off prom
    queens and popcorn girls, and as the storm clouds swarm
like killer bees, I'll be searching for my Tiny Tim,
    om mani padme om, God bless us, every worm.

Notes

Section I

The epigraph, "Breviary" by Zbigniew Herbert, is translated here by Barbara Hamby and Dominika Wrozynski.

Mambo is derived from the Bantu word meaning "conversation with the gods." The mambos in this section are my conversations with my own personal gods, which I picture as less like the great monotheistic deities and more like the Greek gods: quarrelsome, backbiting, sentimental, and prone to sexual fiasco.

Two of the poems in this section and the title poem of the book are written in a form that I probably didn't make up, but I'm fairly sure I made up the name. I call them double-helix abecedarians because I'm entwining two alphabets, one at the beginning of the line and one at the end.

"Ode to Laundry, Lester Young, and Your Last Letter" is for Lynn Fiedeldey.

Section II

This section is a sequence of poems that I call abecedarian sonnets. Again I'm working with the beginning and ends of the lines. There's one poem for each letter of the alphabet, each poem except one opening with its title letter and then following the alphabet through the poem. I decided to use this particular configuration because so few English words end in "q," "j," or "v." I thought I might be able to come up with thirteen words ending in "j" but not twenty-six.

Section III

During a semester in London, I spent many hours in the British Library reading about Pindar's and Horace's odes. As a result, I wanted to try to construct a more formal ode in the manner of these two poets, but also a poem that incorporated Pindar's wild associations and Horace's intimacy yet still had the syntax and diction of a twenty-first-century mind. Some of the odes are closer to Pindar and others to Horace, but I owe these poets an immense debt of gratitude as I do to Keats and Neruda. I also owe a debt of gratitude to Joseph Brodsky and Andrew Marvell. These poems would never have taken their present form without obsessive immersion in two especially gorgeous poems by these two poets.

Acknowledgments

Acknowledgment is made to the following journals in which some of the poems in this collection first appeared, sometimes in earlier forms:

Blood Lotus ("Elizabeth Cady Stanton Writes the Dictionary"); *Boulevard* ("All-Night Lingo Tango" and "Who Do Mambo"); *Café Review* ("Lysistrata Lectures the Gods" and "Ode on Diagramming Sentences in Eighth-Grade English Class with Moonlight, Drugs, and Stars"); *Cimmaron Review* ("Ode to White Peaches, Pennies, Planets, and Bijou, the Dog"); *Five Points* ("Mr. Nollie Hinton Talks to Me While I Test Drive His 1955 Studebaker," "Ode on My 45s, Insomnia, and My Poststructuralist Superego," "Some Days I Feel Like Janet Leigh," "Plead My Cause, Max von Sydow," and "What Profit Is There in Being Marlene Dietrich"); *Iowa Review* ("Whatever or As You Like It, Part II"); *Indiana Review* ("Ode to Airheads, Hairdos, Trains to and from Paris"); *Nightsun* ("The Fool Hath Said in His Heart," "Hear My Prayer," and "I Beseech Thee, O Yellow Pages"); *Ocho* ("Hope Revived: The Road to Baghdad" and "Ode to Little Boys"); *Pool* ("Mambo Cadillac" and "Ode on Cake, Catcalls, Eggs with a Minor Scary Reference to the End of the World"); *Quarterly West* ("So Says Cleopatra, Reincarnated as a Hippie Chick, Circa 1968" and "Ulysses Discusses the Underworld with Freud"); *River Styx* ("O'ahu Mambo" and "Ode to Fear"); *Runes* ("Friday Slams Crusoe"); *Salmagundi* ("Examine Me, O Lord, For I Have Loved," "I Will Praise You, Constance Bennett," "My Heart Cleaveth Unto Such Trash" and "Working at Pam-Pam's"); *Spring Formal* ("Olive Oyl Discusses Quantum Theory"); *Subtropics* ("Ode on Dictionaries"); *storiesSouth* ("Venus and Dogberry: A Match Made in New Jersey"); *TriQuarterly* ("Betty Boop's Bebop," "Karen, David, and I Stop in Front of the Pitti Palace," "Ode to Anglo Saxon, Film Noir, and the Hundred Thousand Anxieties that Plague Me like Demons in a Medieval Christian Allegory," "Ode on Laundry, Lester Young, and Your Last Letter," "Ode on the Letter M," and "Zeus, It's Your Leda, Sweetie Pie,"); *Verse* ("Aloha, Dad, Au Revoir, Goodbye," "A Birdman to You, Baby," "Caliban Passes His Driving Test on the Ninth Try," "Desdemona Resuscitated by Sir John Falstaff, EMT," "Ganymede Dreams of Rosalind," "I Find an Entrance to Hell," "Jane Austen Rewrites Hamlet with Interruptions by Russian Poets," "Nietzsche Explains the Übermench to Lois Lane," "Punk Puck or Robin Goodfellow with Fender Stratocaster," "Queen

Mab Blues," "Titus Woos Titania," "Xerox My Heart, Three-Headed Dog," and "Yorick's Soliloquy"); *Waccamaw* ("Razkolnikov Rates the Plays").

"Some Days I Feel Like Janet Leigh" was on Poetry Daily (March 7, 2006) and in the anthology *Poetry Daily Essentials 2007*. "Ode on Dictionaries" was on Poetry Daily (December 13, 2007).

"I Beseech Thee, O Yellow Pages" was in *Poetry Calendar 2007,* Alhambra Publishing, Bertem, Belgium. "Zeus, It's Your Leda, Sweetie Pie" was in *Poetry Calendar 2008,* Alhambra Publishing, Bertem, Belgium.

As always, I must give David Kirby my love and devotion for creating a poetry paradise wherever we live and for making it evident every day that the poetry store is always open. I'm grateful to magazine editors who have taken a chance on some of the wackier formal experiments here, especially Andrew Zawacki at *Verse,* Susan Hahn at *TriQuarterly*, Stephen Dunn in his issue of *NightSun,* Richard Burgin at *Boulevard,* Judith Taylor in *Pool,* CB Follet and Susan Terris of *Runes,* and Peg Boyers at *Salmagundi.* And thank you Charlie Stratton for telling me about Mr. Nollie Hinton's Studebaker dealership. Tony Hoagland's poem "Hate Hotel" has been a continual inspiration to me. Thanks, Tony.

I'd also like to thank Florida State University's International Programs for making travel possible, especially Jim Pitts—the most generous of directors—and Mary Balthrop in London, Ignacio Messina in Valencia, and Sue Capitani in Florence.

This book is dedicated to Phyllis Moore, who has read my poems from the very beginning, helped me choose the right words, and told me in the kindest way possible when I have chosen the wrong ones. I could never have put this book together without her radiant intelligence, tender heart, Wildean wit, and the pleasure she takes in the general nuttiness of life.